ANGRY BIRDS
THE BIG GREEN
DOODLE ★ BOOK

Angry Birds
Big Green Doodle Book

Illustration by Ruska Berghäll
Cover design and layout by Anne-Marie Vesto

ISBN 978-952-276-003-6
Printed in Canada

AMUSEMENT FOR THE KING

A BUCKETFUL OF FUN

WHAT'S EATING YOU?

MOONLIT ISLAND

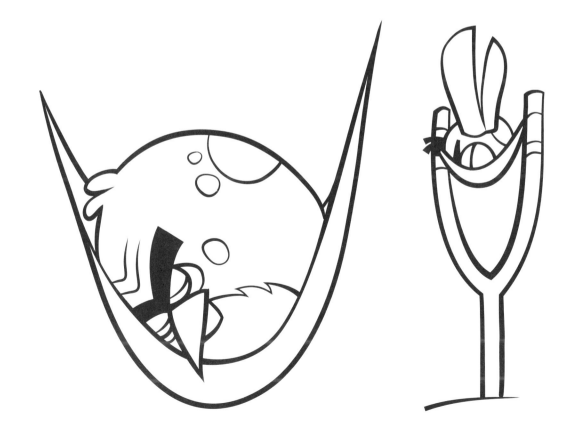

EGGTACULAR ROCK SHOW!

UP, UP AND AWAY

IS THE SIZE RIGHT?

ROOM FOR A MUSHROOM

A STRANGE STEED INDEED

GARGANTUAN BEAK

TOTEM

ANGRY SNOWMAN

HEAVENLY HAVEN

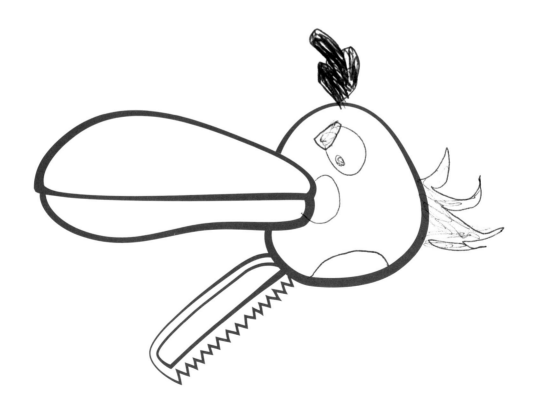

YOU DARE CHALLENGE ME?!

FLYING KITES

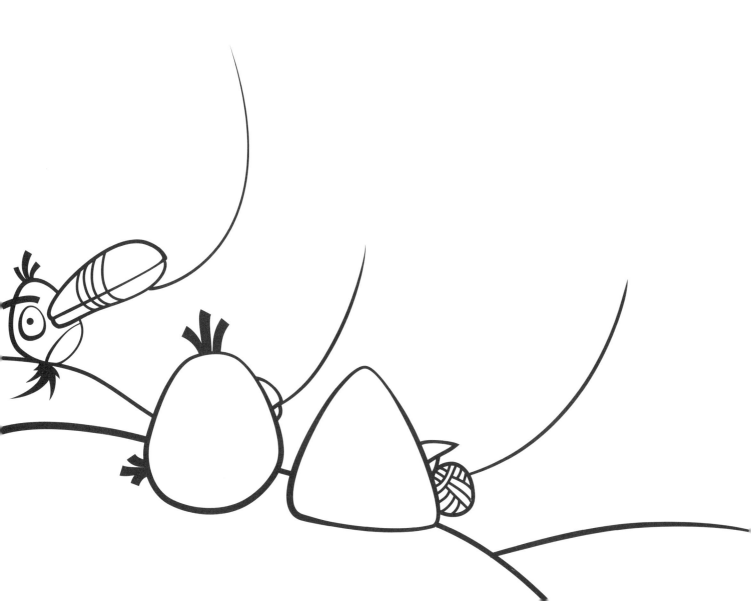

DROP IT HERE

ANGRY BIRDS PILLOWCASE

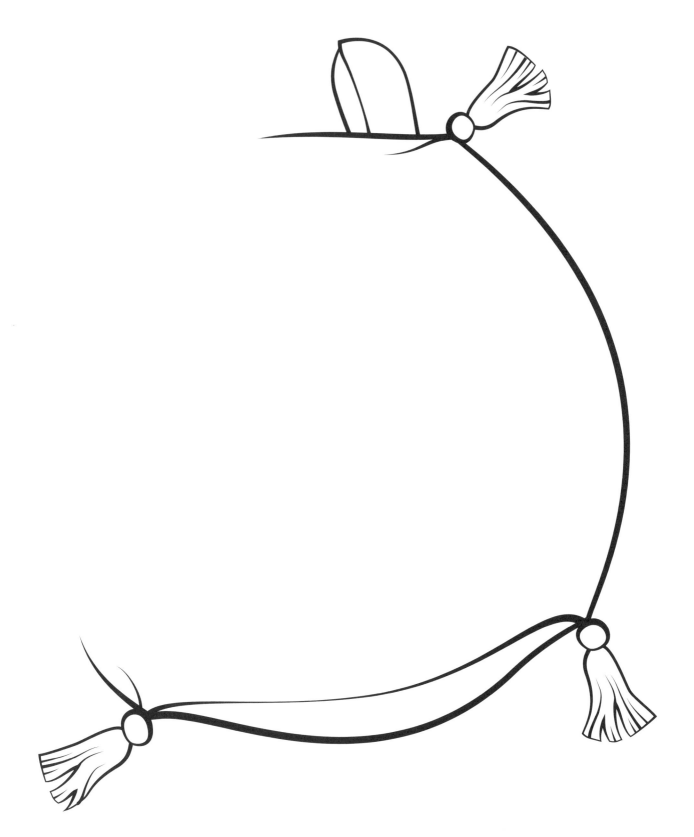

WHO STOPPED BY?

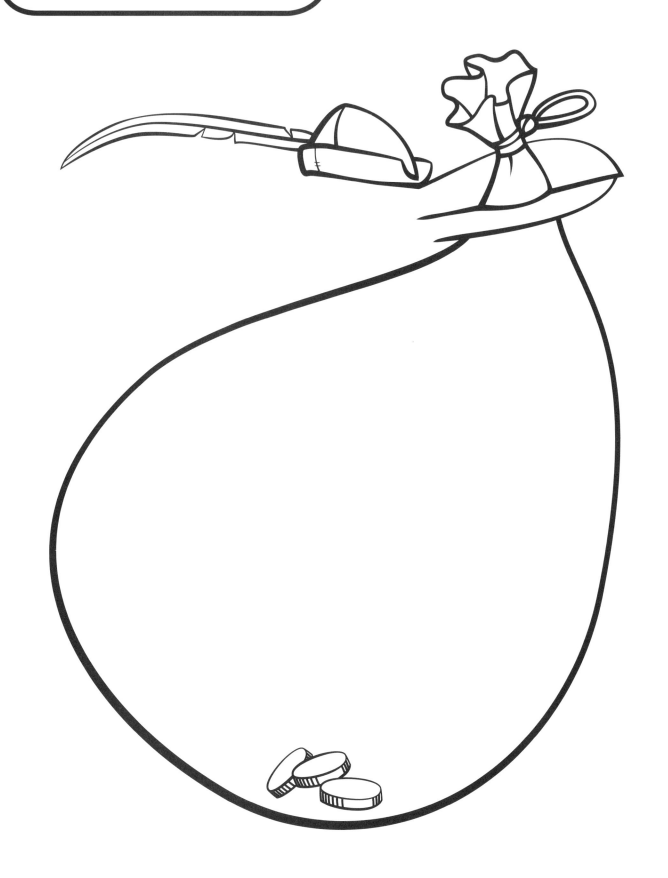

A COMPLEX STRUCTURE

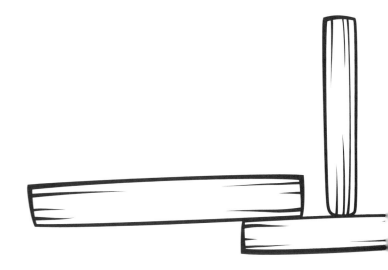

THIS IS HOW I DECORATE

MECH-BIRD IN THE MAKING

I WASN'T FISHING FOR THIS!

A SEA OF BIRDS

WINNER TAKES IT ALL

WANT TO BE FRIENDS?

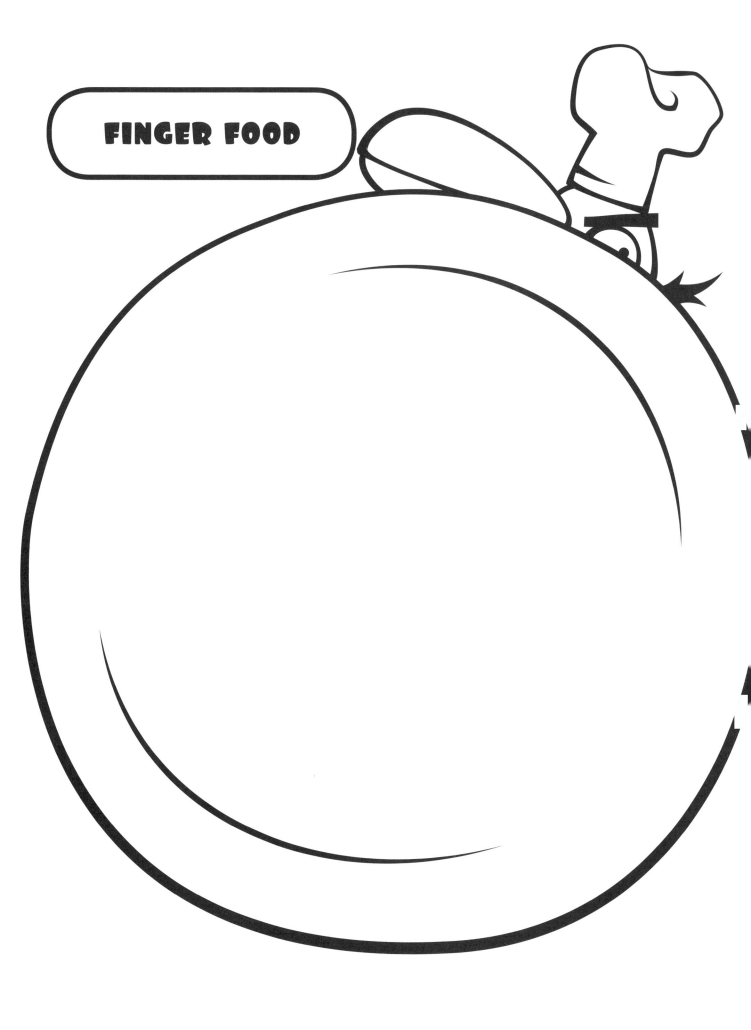

A KING BIRD?

EGGSHELTER

BREAKFAST FOR THE KING

WANDERING CLOUDS

ON THE TRACK TEAM

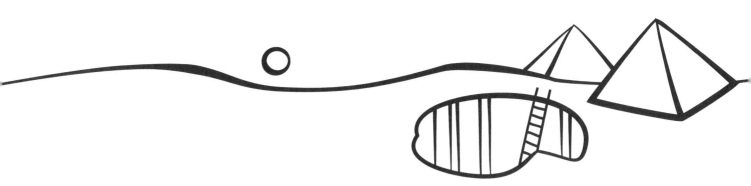

THE ANCIENT CURSE

CATCH A BEAKFUL

FISH TANK

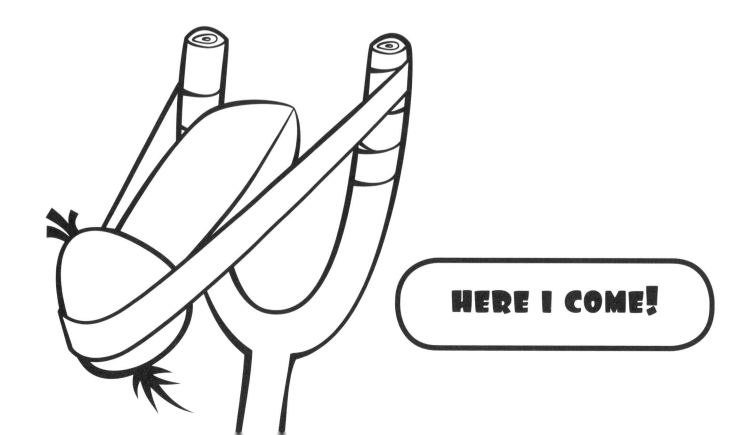

HERE I COME!

WHAT'S IN A BEAK?

THE WRONG EGG

A STUDY IN GREEN

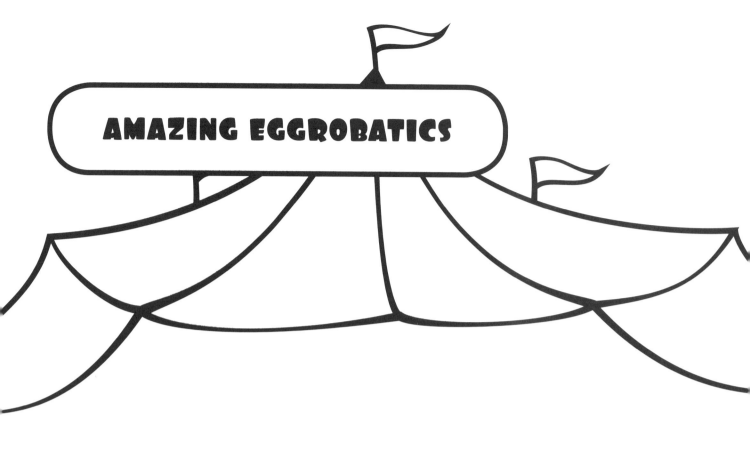

AMAZING EGGROBATICS

A FRIEND LENDS A HAND

ON THE ROAD

HYPERBIRD!

IS THIS ART?

BRANCHING OUT

A FLOCK OF BIRDS, ONE PIG

SUPER-SIZE BURGER

BEST-SELLING STORY

GIGANTIC SLINGSHOT

DRIVING A BIKE (DON'T ASK HOW)

MY SPLENDID COLLECTION

COAT OF ARMS

BAD PIGGIES IN DISGUISE

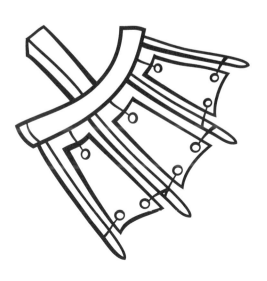

FUTURISTIC DESIGN

SLEEPING BEAUTY

PICKLED EGGS

MESSAGE FROM ANGRY ANCESTORS

BIRDIE OF THE LAMP

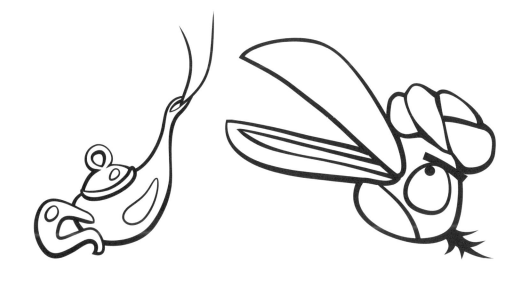

ENVIOUS NEIGHBOR

PLAN B!

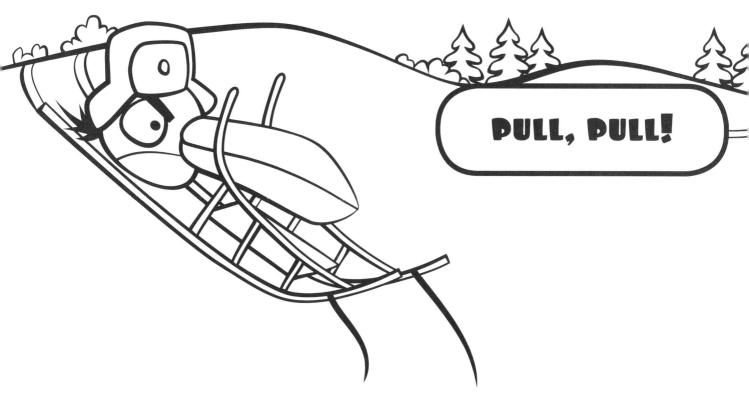

BUZZARD WIZARD

ROUND-TRIP TICKET

BALANCING ACT

STARS FOREVER

WINNER TAKES IT ALL

AN EGG ON A CELLULAR LEVEL

DIFFERENT SLINGSHOT

INCUBATION IN SPACE

SHAPES IN THE SKY

LOCK-DOWN!

MAGIC TREE

 Red

THE BALLOON LOON

LATEST INNOVATION

STRANGE HARVEST

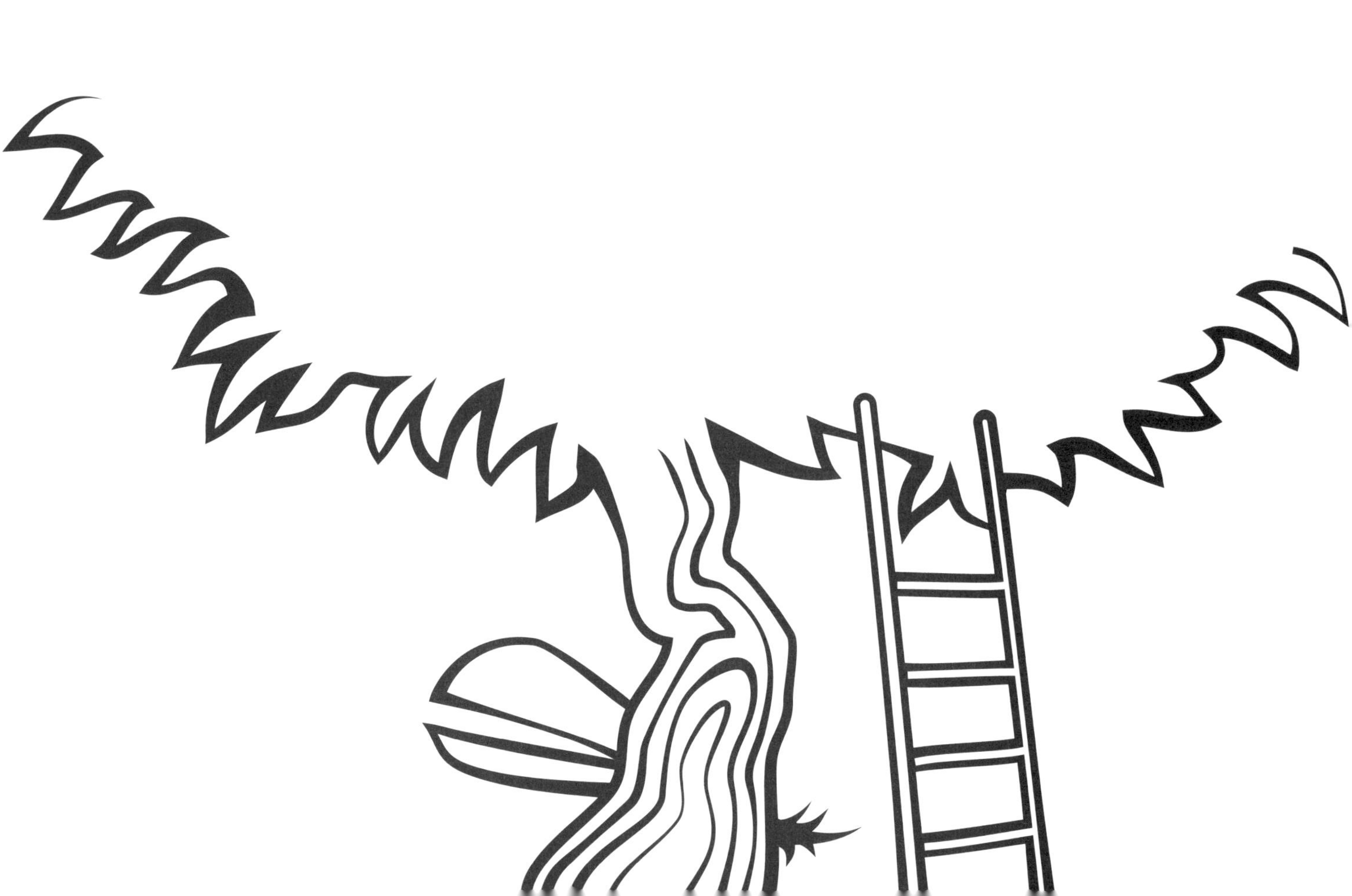

THE WORLD'S HIGHEST BIRDCOASTER

LET THERE BE CAKE!

BEAKS AT THE BEACH

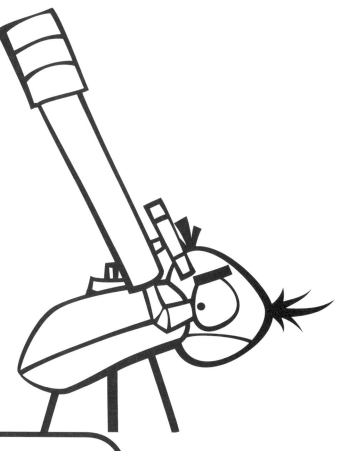

NEW CONSTELLATION
(OF THE MIGHTY EAGLE?!)

LISTEN TO ME, LITTLE ONE!

THE PRECIOUS EGG

MIND-BOGGLING EGG JUGGLING

If you liked this, you might also like

THE BIG RED DOODLE BOOK

The Big Red Doodle Book contains
100 imaginative and ingenious doodles
that will provide you hours of fun!

THIS IS MY CHOICE!